Icicles

On Christine's Front Porch

P. W. Lea

Acknowledgements

To give credit where credit is due,
It was my sister, Mary Louise Murphy,
Who suggested that I write
Something nice (and short).
"Like what?" I asked.
It was winter and there were Icicles outside.
"How about something on... Icicles," the always
Happy Camper said.
"Humph," was my only audible reply.
So here is your request,
Maybe not as nice as you would like.

The Christine in the title is Christine Wall,
The Queen of Wands at Poetry in the Brew.

I also need to thank Klyd Watkins,
Who was there at the beginning, middle and end,
Who freely gave his valuable wisdom and assistance.
Dr. Patricia Waters, who is never a coward when it
Comes to speaking her mind.
Finally, Les Wuescher, who helped with the final push.

There are many others, more than I can remember.
But to all that had to listen to my poetry... thanks.

Contents

Welcome to Icicles

Or how do you do, Mr. & Mrs. Polyp.
Oh, you are unfamiliar with the word?
It is a zoological term for any animal with a fixed base,
Not that any zoologist would ever consider
An Icicle to be an animal, but then
Icicles do consider all zoologists to be weird, in fact
Icicles consider all humans to be weird animals,
Powerful and destructive, but weird just the same,
Their sole purpose the annihilation
Of all other life forms.
But then since humans do not consider Icicles to be
A life form, it is no big loss to them is it?
But the welcome mat is out / and that's never a bad thing.
One other word of caution.
Humans should not have their feelings hurt
If Icicles seem cold and aloof / It is in their nature
Part of the self-preservation thing / a part they feel
Is missing in humans and makes them so different
From every other life form.

1

If you are interested,
And I doubt that you are,
Icicles talk bitterly of betrayal and sabotage.
Oh, by talk I mean the cryptic sentences
Imprinted outwardly on the ice.
"Pair. Pain. Lookers. Not one small."
Make of it what you want,
It is only there for a moment,
Then inwardly it recedes, eventually disappearing.
But for that moment it is very eerie, emotive.

At first, I thought it was a clumsy attempt
At some avant-garde French gibberish.
Later, and I should be honest with you,
It was the instant success of text messaging
That gave me a hint, perked my interest
Such that I began to correlate the similarities,
Sensing something different was happening.
Not a failed conversation as I had originally supposed
But an opening gambit / a sly nonconfrontational
Statement, and what was needed from me
Was some real discernment / defining words not by
Definition, but by the multiple stages from which
Thoughts coalesce / Thus in this whole enterprise,
Which I hope you look favorably upon,
I want the ambiguity to speak for itself.
Therefore, some tolerance will be required.

2

A variation of raucousness exists
In the water colors under the sky.
Within the welter
The weltschmerz (velt-shmertz)
(Oh, you don't speak German)
The sorrow, the disillusionment, the uneasiness.
This pain is caused by contemplating the troubles
Of this world which, in the case of Icicles,
Is often accompanied by a reluctant acceptance
That they have no other choice.
So it is with so many small atoms who bid
Friend and foe alike, "May I please come with you.
The sky is so dark / and I am so afraid.
If we join / oh please let us join. Together we can survive."
So together the molecules do join / bond as it were
Becoming one / becoming wet and moist,
A liquid like no other.

Now from the West Indies to the Cape,
From the Greater and Lesser Antilles
To the North Shore and South Boston,
A great storm is brewing / And humans being humans,
Being smart, go inside for their own safety.
The kettle hisses and tea is served,
For humans are a well-known people,
Known to be well-spoken, well-kept, and well-grounded,
But outside, it is a Kibitzer
(Oh, you don't speak Yiddish),
A free-for-all, a melee, a riot up and down the line.
"Watch where you are going / Slow down over there
Don't go so fast / Try and hold on to the spot where you
land

Don't splash / Never splash /
You will make a mess of yourself."

Now further down south
Puddles are being made
Streams are forming, and creeks are on the rise,
But up north there is a glaze
In the air, a white, silvery, fluffy glaze
Everywhere. There are many variations
As to what happens next, but one thing
Is for sure: Icicles are formed
And there is nothing you or I can do about it.
The strange part of this story,
The part the Icicles do not find amusing
In the least, is that while Icicles are growing
Outside, solid and sturdy,
Humans, the ones tucked safely inside,
Have come out and are now running amok.
"Look everyone it is snowing,"
And immediately snowballs are flying
And snowmen are being made.
It is chaos, total chaos out there. And the Icicles
Are thinking, "I left home for this!"

3

At-t-t / Ah-t-chu
Don't even think it.
Icicles don't sneeze
Nor do they cough
Nor do they spread germs.
Humans do,
So don't go blaming Icicles
When you come down with a cold.
Icicles are specially made,
Frozen solid,
Hermetically sealed,
No Kleenex needed.
I know, it's not fair,
Icicles outside all day, taking it in
While you're inside fighting off a cold.
Don't go blaming Icicles
Because they are winter's favorite child,
You fair beauty,
I never see you crying that Icicles are not around
Come summer when you tan and swim / go out and
Get bitten by all the bugs, snakes and other small critters.
Oh, did you step in some poison ivy? How sad.
Oh, I believe I omitted Band-Aids.
Icicles would never be caught dead wearing a Band-Aid.

4

As favorites of the gods
Or should I say goddesses,
Mankind was blessed until Prometheus
Stole the secret of fire.
As for Icicles, to be honest,
The gods showed little interest.
They were never anyone's plaything,
Were never selected to be anyone's favorites.
Always under the radar,
Icicles played no significant part
In the founding of the modern world.
But do not cry, at least not for Icicles.
That ancient thievery has at last played out
And the querulous gods seem a lot less content
With their unruly children / now that they have developed
Weapons of the nuclear, biological, and chemical kind.
Always spoiled, and accustomed to having their own way,
The gods say they have gotten too big for their britches
And a rude awakening might be in store.
So what do you say now,
Proud Prometheus, now that you have seen
The fire you stole grow wild and out of control?

5

Come with me
And I will let you see
A juxtaposition of sight and sound,
A harangue carefully orchestrated,
A language skillfully integrated into curious materials
All candidly soft-spoken / so that you barely hear a word
When it says, "I am finished here, my work is done."
This is how nature goes about its daily business,
Not with any harsh outburst or intimating clamor
But with a quick, clean stroke / so uncomplicated
That it would go by unnoticed unless it was seen.
But then why would we see it when nothing was heard.
No burgeoning vibrato / No loud rhythmic crack.
In this slick, cool structure / all we see
Is what was broken / an outlying manuscript of ice,
A composition from heaven, quietly left here on earth.

6

A strong point in Icicles is that
They are resistant to any and all
Therapeutic treatment.
There is no psychological analysis
No Gestalt therapy
No EST
No motivational speeches
No reconditioning for the Modern Age.
Weird as it may seem to us
Icicles are happy just as they are.
I believe there are many reasons for the abnormality.
Congeniality might be one,
The absence of any selfish gene might be another
Or maybe, just maybe
Nature was playing around / experimenting
And viola / Icicles.
Unfortunately, nature forgot exactly how they were made.
The important fact here is year after year, eon after eon,
Icicles keep returning / Not that anyone really cares.
In our own selfish little way, we are happy to see them go.
Springtime is the season we humans love best.
Why then did Mr. Eliot say,
"April is the cruelest month"?
Surely, he was not talking about the absence of Icicles.

7

According to Icicles
Travelers should never double back,
Never carry the same load to the same place
That they had visited before / and most specifically
Once their journey is on the way, they should never forget
That the road they are on now / they have been on before.
So I am thinking
All of this sounds familiar,
Not unlike Aeneas and the Golden Bough.
There, Mistletoe was needed
So as not to return / like you were before.

8

For an Icicle,
When the pendulum that has worked so well
For oh so long has stopped,
So too has any thought of hesitation.
The cessation of momentum that has forged
All faith now releases a new strength,
That the roadway arcing downward
Is a pathway leading to a perfect circle
Where the light that is sucked into darkness
Merges through the eye of a needle
And can be seen from the opposite side.
The rushing wind has lost its ferocity,
Leaving all else emphatically still
So that all matter that was so pertinent before
Has lost its cause, its reason, its rationale,
Leaving Icicles free of any earthly bond.
Some Icicles will say, without knowing for sure,
They could see the successor of themselves ascending,
While others, originally more skeptical, say that
Change may very well be like that
Or then maybe we will never know
This force behind the pendulum's swing.

9

I think it was Walter Winchell
Who called Icicles a thrilling bore
Or was that a chilling chore.
Anyway, it was one man's opinion of Icicles
And one of the best things about Icicles is
They don't care / They are impervious to insults /
To wisecracks / To ostracism / To the cold shoulder.
Icicles come and go as they please
Without so much as a by your leave.
They are not beholden to anyone.
Look at it from their point of view,
Glaring down from 15 or 20 feet,
Keeping an eye on the clouds / their nose in the wind.
Right quick you are going to figure out what is important
And someone else's estimation of your situation
Counts for nothing / Icicles know without being told
That if your last name is Sherman / and your title is General,
Georgia is not a good place to be visiting.
So you take care of your business
And Icicles will do just fine by themselves
You tater head / apple cheek / two legged lopsided claptrap.

10

For mankind
Obstacles arise out of nowhere.
Annoyed at first, only later do we look
To the sky to ask why / why us?
For Icicles, obstacles do not arise,
Rather occur as invitation,
Brilliant and from the East
They shine, often brightly
But always unassuming.
Nothing unexpected is happening here.
This explains the differences in their responses,
For man's forces are collected / plans laid out,
A challenge is to be met / For Icicles
They are happy to see a new day has come.

Icicles are gifts and are the preamble to gifts.
They are gifts of coherence and control.
They are gifts of felicity on a cold winter's morn,
A gift we are scarcely prepared for.
Icicles see themselves as gifts that
Humans are unsure whether to accept.

Icicles know for a fact that
People are not like Icicles,
That we murmur / that we talk and chat.
We argue and disagree / We fight.
Icicles are as quiet as an evening in Vermont,
Are slightly disheveled and oblong.
They know they are remarkably delicate, yet have
The audacity to stay outside and stand on their heads
All winter, a feat they see as commonplace. But also a feat
They think is important, a feat Icicles feel we humans
Would do well to study. Therein is the gift
Icicles long to give. Humans, being humans,
Do not always see things in such a thorough manner.

After much discussion, a conclusion was reached,
Not by one and all, but by enough so that it was made clear
That we humans believe Icicles, while commendable
For their tenacity, are of little to no value.
Icicles could not understand / This is how we were raised,
Believing Icicles stood outside in the winter
Only to gain our attention,
Only so we would spend time and money
Admiring them. Therefore, to humans, these gifts
Are totally unacceptable. Please close
The door behind you, and do not bother to return.

Most Icicles were raised on a platform
High above the norm / and that is why they have always
Seen things differently / and what they've seen of humans,
Well, none of it is very nice. They see humans as huge,
Ponderous, coarse, and slapdash.
They see humans as fragmentary in nature,
And most notably psychologically unfinished.
They say we are an aggregate of the profane
That has failed to evolve into the sacred.
Still, Icicles believe their gifts might help.
So every winter they leave them outside
Our doorstep. And every winter they are ignored
Or worse, called a bore. And if they vanish for good
I am afraid humans will not fret over it one bit.

12

Icicles chronicle each drop
From the footbridge / where they first learned to joist
To the parcel of earth no larger than a pin drop
Where information they have gathered over a lifetime
Is carefully deciphered / the hermetically sealed lock
Is broken / letting the water like school children run
Out and play in exhalation / in improvisation / in
Nearly perfect salutation they saturate the earth.

13

When Icicles dissipate
They do so lily white.
When they dissolve
It is as an opaque pearl.
Why maneuver in such a way
When Icicles know it makes little sense
To stay as you are
now that you have gone.
It is the Earth's green mantle,
This colorful parade which Icicles have come to join.
It tells them to come as you are,
A request to which Icicles happily comply.
No groundbreaking research here.

In the vernacular of Icicles'
Equilibrium is the
Crocodile in the tub,
The alligator in the pool,
The cry of the Banshee / the laughter of the gods,
The vibes in "Good Vibrations,"
The crucifix on the Crusader Shield,
The crotch in the Jock Strap.
It is Thor's hammer / Superman's cape.
It is the magic in the illusion,
The land of milk and honey,
The vestibule to Mount Vesuvius,
The Fort in Fort Oglethorpe,
The Goose in Goose Bay.
Without equilibrium, all bets are off.
The Gorilla won't be able to ride the tricycle,
The spaceship will not land on the moon.
With equilibrium, all else is good.
Without equilibrium, all else counts for nothing.
If I walk, letting one foot follow another,
There will be no applause.
But let me fall, the laughter will teach me
To watch my step / This is not the case with Icicles.
There is no trial period / no watch and learn.
There is only do / and once done stay strong.

15

Mystics were the first to study Icicles.
Their conclusion was that "Icicles are the body
And soul of water. A god different from all others."
Next came the alchemists / Their mission was different.
They were searching for gold / the power to turn other
Elements into gold, and their conclusion about Icicles was,
"Icicles were the weapons of some long-ago vanquished god
Who had sought to dominate the earth but was thwarted
So he hid in the winter where the sun was weakest.
Thus, Icicles are the relics of his power and
Should not be fooled with unless humans
Wish to feel the wrath of his ire."
What Icicles saw in both of these ancient treatises
Is a fact Claude Levi-Strauss so ably pointed out:
"Man's insistence on the right
To name and define the world about him."
Icicles began their study of man at a much later date.
The reason for this is obvious. "Why bother?"
Up until the Industrial Age, man was considered
More a nuisance than a threat. Now, Icicles have compiled
Thousands and thousands of documents concerning man.
Most read like the script from a horror movie. However,
One does agree with Mr. Strauss: "Modern man would do
          well
If he would take the time to learn from his ancestors.
Not so much in how they saw the world, but in how they
Saw themselves in this world."

16

Twice, maybe even a few times more,
Mostly when there is a Good-Humor cart below
And the ring-a-ling sound from its bells
Lifts them up / suggesting a thousand new meanings
To winter's solitary performance / or then, maybe
Every once-in-a-while / when in the woods
A young man traipses along / reciting Longfellow's
"Song of Hiawatha" in a voice that could be
The voice of Longfellow himself /
Do Icicles feel happy.
I don't think I am breaking any new ground here.
We all know Icicles are a long way away
From our hectic, highfalutin' lifestyle,
But we never think of them as unhappy
And they are not / not as we are on winter's days
When we swear there's nothing left good to do.

17

Icicles hover into antiquity.
The process of civilization
That emerged and transformed much of the world
Eluded Icicles, and as a result
Icicles are a force unlike any other.

Culturally and spiritually, Icicles are stocked
With the dialect of ancient wisdom.
The most comprehensive exploration of this issue is
How Icicles Saved Civilization, Volumes I, II, III, & IV
Which clearly states,
"Icicles' ability to mysteriously vanish,
Then reappear at a different time and place
Untouched, exactly the same as before, straight forward
Without any discernable changes in patterns is unique,
Making Icicles an important topic
In the study of nonlinear history."

About all of this shilly-shally, Icicles say, "Poppycock,"
Or maybe, more appropriately, "We beg to differ."
"Our business," Icicles calmly explain, "has always
Been out in the open, in the public eye, giving us little
Chance for any shenanigans. Ok, an evening out
with the guys, a few pints, one or two quick games of
        pinball.
But that is it. Next morning is work as usual.
Try to imagine if your entire mental and intellectual life was
Form-fitted into a preset design that is not only precarious,
But pointed in the opposite direction to any real concerns
You humans might hold dear. Stop being so suspicious
And start giving us an even break. Icicles are here
To be enjoyed, not idealized or demonized."

This is pretty much word for word
What Icicles think of humans.
True, there is some exasperation, some hyperbole,
But then Icicles believe humans like to blow things up
Out of all sense of proportion.

In the Mythology of Icicles,
A body of work that covers many centuries
It was a body of water that first complained
About how fast-flowing their journey was,
Massive amounts of waters rising and ebbing.
All of this left them feeling
Unnoticed as a single entity.
The gods who themselves are immeasurable / laughed,
Saying, "As a whole you are one of the most powerful
Forces we have yet created, now you want
To be single and free."
Still unhappy, the water roared and stormed,
Flooding most of creation, so that the gods had to relent
And Icicles were made, just so the water would be pleased,
All single drops / all like-minded / all free. But the gods
Have a mind of their own, and never appreciate being
Told what to do / so a caveat was added / a strange twist /
That dictated only in winter could this magic be seen /
Too late the water's simmer / What was done was done /
Only in winter would Icicles stand out different and bold /
The rest of the year, which was most of the time,
The water would fall as solitary raindrops / For this is how
The gods are when granting wishes / A little for you
The rest for them to do as they please / That means
Wine for them / Water for men and their beasts.

19

More than anything else
Icicles are enthusiastically silent,
Especially if you consider they are
Almost always high strung (which they are) and
That they probably have a screw loose somewhere
(A sure bet, for they are always falling off the edge).
So I have been wondering,
Do you think Icicles have seen
Too many Louis Brunnel movies?
"I've got it. In this scene no one says a word.
Wait / Wait / How about in the whole movie
No one says a word."

Or maybe Icicles believe they are actors
In one of Artaud's Theater of the Absurd plays.
"Ok, everyone in this scene,
I want you to stand there and look down.
The whole time when you are on stage, I want
No dialogue, no expressions; just look intently at the floor.
Wow, that will put the audience on the edge of their seats.
The anxiety will have them buzzing.
There might even be a riot,
Oh, wouldn't that would be wonderful."

Or might it be that the alibi Icicles have concocted
Doesn't hold water.
So instead of convicting themselves further,
The Icicles choose to remain silent.
I can see it now,
A hard sweat pouring off the faces of Icicles,
Yet no matter how much the authorities turn up the heat,
The Icicles refuse to crack. "Some real cool customers,

These Icicles," the police say in disgust.
"Maybe we got the wrong fellows."

Yes, I understand now why Icicles are so quiet:
Without sound, there is no chance of identification.
A bark or a meow is a sure giveaway
That a cat or a dog is around.
But when the screen goes quiet, it is anybody's guess
As to what is on the other side of the door.
With silence, there is not a hint or suggestion
As to who or what is out there.
Not too shabby, Icicles / very stealth-like.
I like it / you being the mystery hiding in plain sight.

20

Icicles have become truly distressed
Over any suggestion
That they are on some sort of a collision course.
Look, folks, for long periods of time,
Eons upon eons,
Icicles have hung in there.
True, they were upside down,
True, they were staring straight in the face of doom.
And Icicles will tell you
The effect on their psyche was horrible.
However, that did not mean
Suicide was right at the top of the list of things
Needed to do today / Just the opposite.
They got down to business / Became better Icicles.
An avoidance strategy? / Well maybe, yes,
But then what would you have them do all day / drool?

21

The idea that Icicles are Nature's "happy accident"
Resonates within a small community of Icicles.
Unofficially, these Icicles are referred to as the "Smilers."
This is to be expected. After all, they are
The most ephemeral of Icicles
And are known to break off at any hint of meliorism.
Or in today's lingo, at any change in the weather.

22

Even the most rudimentary understanding of Icicles
Shows they are not creepy.
Only the very ignorant would consider using that word,
Especially when finding oneself located
Directly below one said creepy Icicle.
Any and all results are to be expected,
The worse being you might look a little creepy
With an Icicle stuck to the top your head.

23

Icicles like to say they are "staying focused"
And use it often in association with the word "undeterred,"
A reference, I suppose, to their surroundings.
I mean it does not take much imagination to guess
The many obstacles faced by Icicles each day,
Hazards truly horrendous.
This leads me to believe that their talk
Gives some insight into their state of mind.
"Oh wow, look at that sunrise, it is a biggie. Stay focused,
Yes, this is me undeterred by the warm glow from the sun.
What a complete exaggeration. A cake walk. This is
nothing,
Absolutely nothing. Stay focused.
Pssssst. Hey, you over there. Are you staying focused?
Hey, where are you going? Don't do that."

24

For those intrigued by opposites,
Here is a doozy.
Icicles seldom succumb to silliness
And are never distracted by enthrallment.
But when it comes to deciding what to do next,
Never was there a bunch more willing to cry out,
"It is now or never" than Icicles.
This is not due to some need for instant gratification,
Nor is it a morbid sense of curiosity.
It is more like an inherited trait by which all Icicles
Are in sync, or worse,
Competitive to see who will be first.

25

In exile
And in disgrace, Cicero
Waits upon an Icicle to fall.
"Lucky the Icicle," Cicero laments,
"It does not know that all of its efforts
Have been for naught."
Icicles love to tell this story,
Then add, "Poor Cicero, did he not know
He was a favorite among the gods?"

26

Drop by drop
An Icicle with one long leg dissolves.
Oh, Don Quixote,
You Man of la Mancha,
Don't you know it is time?
Miracles begin not with the sunrise
But in your dreams where dragons
and windmills are all the same
And a beautiful fair lady, she waits.
Oh, how lucky you are to be a man.
Awake, Don Quixote,
It is time.

Outwardly, Icicles are a centrifugal spiral.
Inwardly, the antecedent is not downward
But earthbound / a total immersion.
I know, the result is the same,
But there is a difference, a very important difference.
To do this, to keep going down / centimeter by centimeter,
Icicles must maintain a sense of growth,
A palpable intention that all of this twisting and turning
Is outwardly invisible / inwardly shining,
An interaction that must be familiar as it is strong,
Capturing trust and generating movement,
All of this while squeezing out the emptiness and the void.
There can be no divided forces here,
No inadequate signals or confused blemishes,
Not even briefly / Sparseness is the mechanics
By which this all works / To this end,
A language is constructed / where words are the cement
To be applied when needed / This sublimation /
This amputation / this streamlining requires Icicles
To be precise / no psychoanalysis / no loquaciousness
About being alone / or how hard and unfair life is.
This is how it is with Icicles and it is all there /
In prose painful and real / written in the ripples /
The curves / and the bows / spoken in the icy drops /
Icicles are our cold companion / a strange bedfellow
Who stays outside our window each wintry morning /
To teach us how to say hello / not to an empty sky
But to an earth who will be our mother for an eternity.

28

So what is heresy for Icicles, you might ask?
To start with, the right attitude might qualify.
Hanging out on a limb,
The right attitude certainly ranks high up there.
It is corrosive / undermining.
It is worse than animosity. With Icicles,
Animosity is just insecurity,
A solemn belief that others have it better.
The right attitude is like a total disregard for gravity.
The right attitude is like saying, you are up here to stay.
And no one / not no how / can change this.
The right attitude is like if you fall / it is not your fault /
And it makes no difference / because you will bounce back.
The right attitude is like a double standard / only worse
Because you screw yourself out of any joy or happiness.
In Icicles, the right attitude is an aberration / a deviation,
The head turned up looking for salvation from above
Instead of looking down at the truth of what is below.
The right attitude is a deception seen as a gift,
Sloppy chicanery / ricocheting bullets.

29

Unlike humans
Icicles never say
Done, finished, completed,
Not in the context by which we humans
Enunciate these words,
Not in the obligation which Icicles attach to them.
A journey one never intended to start
Does not have to end just because
A point on a map has been reached.
Circles can and do overlap,
A journey beginning here
Can pass here over and over again,
Still it is not done / a circle has no finish line.
For Icicles, finished is a false assumption,
A lack of imagination,
A failure to see how all the dots connect.
"He's finished, that was his last drop"
Does not mean work has not started elsewhere.
Conditions have allowed him to move on.
That's all, done for today means just that,
Today I'll never see again.

Beyond question, Icicles are both
Whimsical and odd, and if the truth be told,
These qualities are not to be recommended
For the public at large, or for individuals
Like myself who do not wish
To be thought of as swishy.

Of the two, whims are the worst.
They are not only erratic,
But they can confound all logic.
Dare I say, they are destructive of truth
In its fullness, and where
Is the virtue in that? Yet Icicles persist.

As for odd,
Being odd is the birthright of Icicles.
No application is needed.
They are odd by virtue of their being
Able to hang upside down
Without so much as a by your leave.
The nerve
And achievement they claim is by grace and design.
The nerve
They claim as their primary accent,
And if that is true, then their secondary accent
Is on being whimsical, which I find downright unnerving.

Whims are preoccupied with the whimsical.
Icicles of devotees of manifest destiny.
Just because being whimsical is
The operational definition of being an Icicle
Does not mean they have to hang off of every rooftop.

Look at them up there,
Cool as a cucumber and playing possum,
Then playing the opposite, playing the victim.
When I first heard that, I was speechless.

Icicles are a revolt against the norm.
One's sanity is threatened any time one is seen
Hanging down like the sword of Damocles,
A symbol of disaster if they should waver.
The nerve,
I tell you, Icicles certainly have the nerve.
That is why I call them
Pitchmen for the old switcheroo,
Believing they will have the last say.
Well, it is just plain whimsical if you believe that
And very odd that a lot of people do.

31

For Icicles, all life is overflowing.
Nature's bounty depends upon this simple fact
That there be more than enough
Fields, flowers, streams, trees
In all variety, in all shapes, forms, and colors.
True, Icicles come in one shape, one color,
And one variety, that of being cold,
But also overflowing, such that Icicles happily
Give more than they ever possess.
Thus, Icicles view each lost drop of water
Not as a diminishment, but as a migration,
A voyage outside of themselves whereby
They are known by what they give.

32

Icicles do not see themselves
As a neutral substance with non-essential properties.
An aforementioned glib assessment assigned to them
By man was meant to lower their expectation of
What one may expect / what they are deemed worthy of /
No, Icicles insist their existence is essential
To one and all and this includes man.
This insistence is seen mainly in their location /
Elevated. Not just one or two steps above but elevated /
And this is not to be seen only as a source of power or status
But as a calm reassurance of their lofty purpose.

Icicles are skeptics.
They firmly believe and hold fast to the notion
That events in nature cannot be predicted.
Thus, any predictions concerning any outcomes
Should be viewed with (should I say) skepticism.
It is this fact, or intellectual facility, which provides
Icicles with their tranquility and calm demeanor.
There are rumors of an impending catastrophe.
Icicles are most certainly aware of these rumors,
And, I might add, have been accused falsely
Of instigating them and spreading them
To any and all who would listen. (Unfortunately,
There might be a small portion of truth
To the latter part of this assertion,
But it was done by only a small portion of Icicles
Who had only the highest of intentions.)
Actually, they were afraid that men, being men,
And being slow by nature, might not be able to grasp
The vast implication, not only to Icicles but to all life,
So this paper is to affirm that by nature, Icicles are skeptics,
That Icicles have a deep and abiding faith in nature,
That nature in her course will provide
And there will always be Icicles.
Whether or not man makes it is up for debate.
Certainly, it looks like a long summer ahead,
But winter will eventually return.
And with winter, Icicles.

34

It is common knowledge that for Icicles,
Happiness is contemplation.
Thus, their ability to stand still over a lifetime
Demonstrates either that boredom is happiness
Or that stillness is not necessarily boring.
For most humans, the ability to stand still
For any length of time shows an utter lack
Of anything useful to do. Should I stand still
For that long, I would die of boredom.
The difference explains a lot.

35

There is a common assumption
Among more than a few Icicles
That no evil can come from time
Spent in contemplation. Obviously, Icicles
Have spent little time among humans,
Whose hands are blood-stained
And whose schemes are callous.

Icicles have vitality,
A rhythmic assurance.
In spite of all that man has done,
Icicles know "Winter is still ours."
Icicles know the ivory age is over,
The ice age has melted / Gone are the
Great columns of ice 40 feet wide / 120 feet high,
Formidable not only as decoration
But as a declaration: "We are here to stay."
Gone, too, are their most extravagant designs,
Ice hanging down from the ceiling like guards,
Candlesticks of sculpture-like Icicles 10 to 20 feet long.
Gone after 10,000 years, these once great
Columns of compassion, hope and charity /
This new light that was to refine light
To be the delight of all / this demonstration
Of Icicles' faith in the future for all.
For now, they are a system in decline.
Icicles, who had damned all else as unnecessary
Finally saw their own kind / falling apart, now
Lost in a bizarre and terrifying darkness /
Lost in a relentless reshaping of everything.

No more do Icicles think of man as a work in progress,
No more the high-sounding pronouncements,
"Give men time and they will come around."
The great thaw has begun / And these evil-looking
Evil-acting creatures have decided
To rule alone over the earth for the profit
They may gain / To eliminate any and all
Vestiges of the old world / That the dollar
Will grant all their true value /

Give nature the incentive to do better.
Yet still Icicles arrive each winter,
Still they say, "Hang on." Maybe it is that vitality,
That refusal to play any part in man's plan.
Ever a new beginning / ever crying,
"Our beauty shall not by denied."

37

That Icicles never question
The repetitive nature of their fashion or customs,
The Greek stoics found exemplary. Thus,
The toga was made the only required attire.
Thus, the cowboy, taciturn,
Dressed in tough leather.

An uneven red carpet
With a large golden flower embroidered in the center,
A cream-colored room
And a small suspicious puddle of water off in a corner.
In themselves, the blue curtains offer little possibility
Except that they are left open and have
"Made in Paris" sewed at the bottom.
Icicles are known to follow High Fashion,
But this time, have they gone too far?

39

It is true Icicles are notorious for their silence
But this does not mean they cannot answer
Yes or no questions.

Did you stay out all last night?
A bowed head (a dull sheen) translates as a
"Maybe," as in "Maybe yes or maybe no.
Why do you want to know?"

Were you at the Kit Kat Club?
A single drop sliding off to the right translates as
An interested "Why do you ask / Did anybody call? /
Was it the girl with blonde hair? / I gave her your number."

There was some dampness in the front seat
Of my car / Anybody we might know?
Elbows up (glistening) translates as an excited
"Wow! The jazz was hot, those guys were wailing."
Elbows up with a rapid fall of drops means
"You really missed something last night,
You old guys got to learn to stay up later.
Oh, sorry about your car."

40

Icicles are never clumsy.
Blundering is not what they do.
Being awkward is an embarrassment,
A real nuisance, especially if there are damages.
A smooth style is what Icicles like.
It helps alleviate any difficulties
Getting home after falling down.

41

In all seriousness, Icicles asked
What work of art animated is man?
Mercurius duplex.
In all seriousness, Icicles believe
The left side of man's brain has folded.
Instead of a perfect circular form,
It is a triangular aberration,
Still splendid,
Still able to function,
But not able to produce dreams
That flow in sweet content,
Dreams divinely thought.
Instead, man's dream are two-sided,
With cars and horses dressed in iron,
Dreams of driving over mountains,
Dreams of charging through rivers of water.
Man's art is man's dream,
And what Icicles see in man's art has left them frightened,
Mercurius duplex, man as god, man as the devil,
Man outside of nature looking in.

42

Twenty-eight disappearances,
Each one believed to be foul play.
In the coming years, Icicles have vowed
Due to their ground-breaking research
That those Icicles out on the edge
Should move a little closer to the center,
A tactic our do-nothing congress
Would do well to pick up on.

43

There is so little discrepancy between Icicles,
I don't blame people when they say
Seen one, seen them all,
Know one, know them all.
To tell the truth, the singular thing
That differentiates Icicles is their message
Scrawled in tiny cuneiform:

"Our names are like Chamberlains at the Royal Court.
Our Prince calls, we go and do his bidding."
                                        Reads one,
"The chasm below
Overlooks eternity's solitude.
I am certain that my lack of hesitation
Will scratch one of the rocks below.
I hope what is seen will look obscene,
Then all can be certain it was me."
                                        Another reads,
"A barren winter's night,
The moon is waiting for a crime to occur.
No longer above suspicion,
I think I shall enjoy my rest."
                                        Another,
"I was born here
And below here I shall be reborn.
Unafraid, I come to defend my sweet earth."
                                        Another,
"There is no ceiling in my sky.
When I split,
The sky will show me all of its history.
The moon, the stars,
The planets will move closer

To where my split ends.
That is how I shall greet them
When we meet."

Another,

"Deeper than the earth is the sky
Upstairs, the stars like mineshafts
I must climb deep down.
If not, the light will not follow me."

Another,

"It was a good idea
My coming here.
Now I have my shirttail tucked in
And my buttons all buttoned up.
It is not that I am excited about leaving,
But it is understandable
Even if I don't really understand."

Finally,

"I forgive my dreams
And see now they could never happen.
Forgiving my dreams is my charity
And with charity I shall proceed."

Outwardly, there is little discrepancy between humans,
Only we make such a big deal over any difference
That we fail to notice some of the more important things.

44

The primeval silence of winter's landscape
Captured in a painting is not caused by Icicles.
Nor do Icicles influence our emotions
By the virtue of their solitary solitude
Here and always.
It is our mind which is the determining factor,
And any other explanation tells us
More about ourselves than it does about Icicles.
Yet in the same sequence of fixtures,
This desire to explain a sudden rush of feelings
That have overcome us, Icicles do play a role.
Our thoughts do soften if we await winter's cool breath,
But harden if the presentation is harsh and unforgiving.
Icicles are a sanctioning body.
They allow us to enter their world,
Nothing further from them is needed.
The image which Icicles construct is constant
And it connects uniformly in our mind.
Ahh, have I suggested something here?
That maybe, just maybe, men and Icicles are congenial.
Why, I do believe I have.
If so, why then this war?

45

There has been very little study
Done by Icicles
On the abnormally high send-off ratio,
The time and the amount of heat required
To dislodge a formerly firm and sturdy Icicle.
What used to be thought of as two to three months
Has shrunk to a matter of two to three days,
In some bad cases, two to three hours.
The alarm has sounded, but the research done by Icicles
Has slowed after the initial discovery of the inverse ratio.
The more heat, the less time.
This unwillingness to go further may rest on two or three
Factors, but my gut feeling on this is the sudden abruptness
By which the send-off happens is both
Poignant and disconcerting.
The "yahoo whoooo whoooo whoo I am falllling"
Called out by the sample subject would
Stun and startled the researchers so much / that they
Would fail to collect the necessary data.
I know we see Icicles as cold and hard-hearted,
But folks, this is not the case / and I believe Icicles
Might need some human expertise on this.
Ah yes, the real hard-hearted ones to the rescue.

46

According to Icicles,
What one finds in Webster's is an aberration.
The definitions are lopsided, supporting a vanity
And glory that belongs to men, and men alone.
They are a corruption of the words.
By altering their definition, man has altered the world.

What Icicles want is balance,
A just and true balance,
A world that is more polymorphous
Than Mr. Webster ever guessed
(Even if he did have to guess at its meaning).
Democracy, give nature a break,
Where do you believe man came up with the idea?
Men call their imposing of chaos order,
Then suggest without them everything would be a mess.
The exact opposite is true. And what is worse,
Men put themselves on top of an apex
Which they have the nerve to label as
The Hierarchy of Nature.
Nature has no natural hierarchy,
Rather a chain where every link is of equal importance,
An order based upon how much is given rather than
How much can we get away with / A code of conduct
Men of old celebrated as knightly chivalry, not this
Dionysian orgy we have today. Best of all, in nature there is
A restrictive clause on all creative and destructive impulses,
Not the total war to which man has committed himself,
An enterprise that is destroying and depleting nature's
resources.
All Icicles wish is to be a stepping stone
To help men fulfill their dream / A sustainable society.

47

Among the avant-garde / Icicles lack credentials.
No. I am not making this up. The truly hip believe that
Icicles are "The sole occupants of decrepit fence rows /
Ride on the back bumper of used cars / And live in
The gutterless eaves of abandoned tenement housing."
Not very flattering / but from there it gets worse.
They say Icicles are "Unsubstantial / They carry no weight
And what weight they do carry / it won't hold up."
Wow, that is bad / but they have a point / A lot of what
They say is true / It is all a matter of interpretation /
But what is not a matter of interpretation
Is that they put in print what they had only talked about
Among themselves / Icicles had no choice in the matter /
They did what they had to do / Struck back / Word for word
Keystroke for keystroke / Icicles said that, the avant-garde
hip
"Live in a world machismo self-promoters / A world whose
Detachment from the everyday world is legendary."
So why should Icicles care what they say / Why should
        anyone
Care what they say? Icicles will let the public decide
Who lacks credentials / Who carries no weight.
Unfortunately for Icicles, the public did decide
And that is when I decided to enter the fray / to help bridge
the gap /
Smooth over any misconception. And damn if I didn't get
        run over /
Those effete are a pretty tough crowd /
So to the avant-garde I say, "Go fuck yourself,"
And to the brave Icicles I say, "There are plenty more
Bridges left out there to burn, go step on some toes."

I am astonished / You should be too.
Icicles are binary opposites,
Bland in appearance, yet rich in color,
Narrow in field, but once covered the earth.
They arrive only to dissipate,
To dissolve without any apology /
Without any litany of complaints.
Think of Icicles as a soap bar
And the air outside like our hands,
Cooled and cleansed,
Yet none of this we understand.
What if I told you
Icicles take delight in analytical analysis,
Are the aphelion and the perihelion in orbit.
That they withdrew from summer because
They were not attuned to the weather,
Claim an ancient history
But have little or no ancestry.
They have an asymmetric atavism, which if you don't like,
They suggest that you revert back to Astroturf.
But most of all, they have an abiding hatred
For all of man's inventions /
The ice box and pneumatic drills leading the way.
Icicles have been known to drop at the sight of a drill,
And as for refrigerators they call them
Cheap imitations without the breath of the nature.
Now you are astonished. If not,
Icicles suggest you can go live in the tropics.

49

Being an Icicle demands
A type of restraint not found in men.
With Icicles, there can be no question of resolve.
They cannot say this is wrong or
I would be better off doing something else.
Such thoughts are not permitted.
That is why I was so taken aback
When I noticed on a piece of broken ice the words,
"How dramatic it would be if I swerved
When it comes time for my crossing."
Pirates fly a black flag
With crossed bones and a white skull to announce
To all the world, "Your laws mean nothing to us."
Icicles have no such choice / Without question,
For them, Nature's laws must be obeyed.
This fact alone should tell all men
The order that they are attempting to alter
Is absolute, and should not be tampered with.

50

Being an Icicle
Presupposes some neurosis.
Some of it, I believe, is due to the fact
They leave nothing behind,
No monuments, no graffiti,
No "Leroy was here."
When I mentioned this to Icicles,
This 'now you see us / now you don't,'
This 'dripping, dripping
Now all gone / down the drain /
Vanished / as if you were never here,'

Their reply was magnificent in its vagueness.
"Think of each encounter as a small change
That once it has occurred, the world is not the same."
So I said, "Sounds great,
But what exactly does it mean?"
OK, not so bright on my part.
I guess you could say I was asking for it.
"It means we don't leave behind
Any garbage by the roadside.
No ripped couches / no broken-down chairs
No washing machine left on the front porch,
No old refrigerator left out in the woods,
No old magazines or romance novels
Left strewn about in the back yard,
No rusted-out cars, no worn-out tires,
No toilets, sinks, or plumbing of any kind
Waiting to be hauled off and demolished.
When we leave /
We leave everything pretty much like we found it.
The small changes are

The only product of our encounter with this world,
And we think the world is much the better for it."

Prime example of why one should never ask a question
Unless one is sure of the answer.
So maybe I should have asked,
"You boys missing the Ice Age?
Missing the fact that you moved all of Minnesota
Down to Tennessee,
Leaving Minnesota flatter than a pancake?"

51

"Clinging," Icicles like to say,
Is an acquired attribute.
Being joined together is more than assimilation.
A spur of the moment thing,
Clinging requires some background,
A careful study of make-up.
Then there some ground rules:
You don't start off by saying,
"You sweet little thing you,
I am here for the long haul,
I am here to sweep you off your feet."
It doesn't work that way.
Clinging is all about degrees,
And I am not talking about
The rise or fall in temperature,
But the degree to which you are able to function.
Too hot,
Then there is not a chance in hell.
Too cold,
Then it is impossible to join up.
For Icicles, clinging is art.
When it is done right / it is a beautiful thing,
When it is done wrong / sad if not tragic.
Folks, I think we need to take a closer look at Icicles.
Most of time those boys know how to do it tight.

Elsewhere and Everywhere In-between
Is a starting point in the history of Icicles.
The whole title continues: *in the Center of the*
Circumference:
The Complete Metamorphosis of Icicles.
And no, I have not read the book / My request for it
Was denied / Yet, when you are among Icicles
They quote from it incessantly / calling it
A milestone / monumental in its scope.
Oh wow, all the traditional trademarks of hype.
There is a smaller book, which I did read,
The Luck of Coherence, or Phooey on Parnassus,
And it states that Icicles are / the compliments of dissimilar
Appearances / launched into a storm / where all they owned
Was thrown overboard in confusion / Thus began a
Cohesion / a harmony among two different life forces /
That ruled head and heart / Nothing like it before
Had I ever read / It was simple but held together by the
Beauty of its language / It reminded me of the myth
Of Glaucus / the sea-god who was loved by Scylla & Circe
But then that ended badly / Let's hope with Icicles
A more loving god appears.

53

I am not saying that Icicles
Put a juddering halt to wearing polyester.
Bliss is that dawning to be alive.
All I am saying is throughout the rage,
Not one color photo or sketch done in black & white
Has ever been produced showing Icicles in polyester,
The death knell as its toll is heard not only
By those who care, but by those who might be only
Passing by. The journey from jeans to khakis
Was a bumpy one, and no matter what others may say,
It did stop at polyester.
Misdirected or just plain mean-spirited and insipid,
The layover was miserable, the look was awful,
A gaudy cheapness filled the air.
Of course, there was playful banter about how people look,
But Icicles did the heavy lifting. That cold icy stare
Was like a Kung Fu kick into the jiggling juggling
Mid-section. A joyless look that said,
Joshua did not lead his people out of the desert
to wear polyester. Folks, when it counted most,
Icicles were there for you.
Remember that when you are about to scrape some off
The rear bumper. Your rear bumper could still be there.

54

For reasons good and bad,
There are those who see Icicles as a reckless passion,
A course of action maddening, demonic, and infantile.
This perspective has some validity
Only because Icicles in themselves are so
Unaccommodating / thinking of themselves
As possessing the high ground. "We threaten not,
Thus we will not be threatened."
I keep telling Icicles this is a moral stance
Made from an ethical argument / one which has
No real force in our material world.
But who am I to judge, I who have always seen
Balance as a necessity / asked, when things got so far
Out of whack / what is the best course of action to take?
Then to see Icicles standing alone / past the rage of
Rebellion / coolly, carefully taking a stand /
It has an effect / It made me stop and ask
How now shall we proceed?

55

I am sure you have noticed it,
Or maybe you haven't.
It is not the kind of thing one first notices
Because it is not a big thing.
I mean, we are all here at the same time,
Yet I find it peculiarly striking / Almost fascinating
And next to impossible to guess, to figure out
Which generation Icicles belong to.
Are they Baby Boomers or Generation X?
Every generation has their own peculiarities,
Their own style of dress,
Their own manner of speech.
I like to brag, after one or two sentences,
I can name the year a person was born,
The movies they have seen, or the TV programs they like
(No, I never attempt to name the books they have read,
That is far too personal),
But there are epochs in human time
Most easily identifiable:
Edwardian, Victorian, the Jazz Age
The Lost Generation, those who had to wander off
To Paris to find themselves,
As those of another generation made pilgrimages
To Jerusalem to confirm their faith.
If I could place Icicles in a certain time,
I am sure I could make Icicles a lot more understandable.
But the fact is Icicles are ageless
A condition not found in humans,
But if discovered, could it not be the trait
That unifies us, makes us all a part of this world?

56

Icicles are a middle term,
By summer they shall all be gone.
On that, we can easily agree.
Starting with the study of natural science
There has been a slow and steady return to reason.
Superstition no longer exerts its once strong influence.
In every field, we humans have gained knowledge,
And knowledge is a powerful weapon.
It has made man the most feared creature,
It has given man dominion everywhere.
Still, mistakes were made / To err is not only human
But constant in all endeavors / I believe
We have now reached a middle age,
An age where more reason is required
To help create a world beneficial to us all,
A world that must be if we are to continue
Away from the darkness, the wars that plagued us all,
And it is here where Icicles are a middle term,
Something caught in the middle of two opposing forces.
What reason, why reason, there was never any reason
For Icicles / Why should there be a reason now?
Is this a world where we can say with complete assurance,
This is the world I want to see?
And it's here where Icicles are again the middle term,
A marker between two opposite ends of the pole,
Where we were / and where we want to be.
So it is with science, errors can be made,
But in science, errors can be corrected.
This does not undo the harm, only unarms it.
For every year of my short life,
Icicles have always returned.
Never have I had any reason to suspect they would not.

I fear our children will not be able to say this,
Or say science was mankind's greatest blessing,
Or that it led us out of darkness into the light.
The middle can also be a questioning term,
As in, "what are we in the middle of?"
Here, Icicles dispel any of our concerns:
"We are in the middle of winter
And Icicles have arrived."

I know what you are thinking,
A twist on what Kant would have thought,
"Without humor or good intentions, Icicles are
An insignificant and unspectacular phenomenon."
Well then, thank you for your critique.
I hope the evening was not a total loss.
Maybe for the next act, I should supply
A ventriloquist with his sidekick, a talking dummy,
Never knowing until laughter is heard
Whether the trick or joke had any appeal.
A skillful misunderstanding / the bite of clever words
All combine into something Kant can easily applaud.
Unfortunately for his many believers,
Icicles do not come with a barcode and therefore,
Unlike the talking dummy, their use can be easily
Misunderstood / easily disposed of / but more often
Overlooked as insignificant and unspectacular.
And for the learned man, well, Icicles have one more small
And insignificant lesson for you to learn.
They never had any intention of being any use
To man / none whatsoever,
And that phenomenon alone makes them spectacular.

58

Icicles are adroitly composed
So that any remorse is completely absorbed,
Either that or shed off much like tears,
Not allowed to linger.
In this I feel Icicles are
Much like ourselves,
Burdened by our own mistakes,
Crying out, "What is the use,"
Scorned for trying, forever trying.
What I really like about Icicles:
They concede nothing,
Not even if they are happy.

Icicles are not now or never were
Dyslexic. Think about it for a minute:
Seeing everything backward
While hanging upside down.
Not even Icicles are capable of anything like that.
Reality would be in reverse
With porous gaps in the perception of time.
It is preposterous, the nonsense people will think up.
Of far lesser significances is the fact that
Icicles are androgynous
And see no reason to change,
Sort of a Dutch Door arrangement.
Don't be plucky, it is all very modest
If not downright prudish: one half is open
While the other half of the door is shut closed.
And don't be like Mrs. MacSqueamish's aunt
And ask where the Plimsoll line is.
It is none of your business.
The most important fact here is
Icicles are very comfortable with their lodgings.
Most times both doors are shut
And the window shades are drawn down tight.
How do you like those apples, you pervy perverts?

60

Icicles are often confused.
I believe this confusion can be easily understood as
Due to a certain type of naiveté,
An innocence that seems to be most pronounced in Icicles.
They believe all of what they see to be true,
And if they happen to take in a movie at the drive-in
Or a TV show through a window,
Icicles believe what they see as gospel truth.
When Icicles happen to see Casablanca,
Which to them is certainly not a movie entitled *Casablanca*,
A whole new meaning is granted to the term "fantasy
fiction."

"I could easily live there, Rick's American Café,
And I would have all the Icicles gather around
Singing "Knock on Wood as Sam plays the piano."

"No. It is not like that," I try to explain.
"It is all a set / It is all make-believe."

"You mean there is no cold fog,
No chief of police who enjoys the good life?"

"Maybe? I don't know.
All I know for sure is that
You could not live in Casablanca.
Casablanca is in a desert."

There is a pause / you might even say a pregnant pause
As each Icicle tries to digest what I have said.
Then finally, "Yes, exactly,
That is what everyone keeps telling Rick

When he tells them he came to Casablanca for the waters,
And then Rick tells them he was 'misinformed.'
Are we also being misinformed?"

The movie is not yet over.
Ilse and Victor are flying off into the fog,
Major Strasser has been shot and
Rick and Captain Renault decided
They would make a good pair.
The orchestra has started to play the Marseilles.
It is here the Icicles become glazed over,
And I am thinking, why ruin it for them?
Why should I reiterate that this is pure fiction,
Make-believe and fantasy? That it has
Nothing to do with real life / when in fact
It is by these make-believe stories we become better?

61

Icicles are prone to magisterial pronouncements.
I think this is because, for Icicles,
Everything does hang in the balance.
Equilibrium is their favorite topic.
They have written treatises on the subject,
Equations where every point of pressure is measured,
Tested for tensile strength and stress.
There is a communal wisdom
That has been passed down / some a priori knowledge
Which Icicles regard as historic truth.

I avoid the subject with them completely,
Act as if I don't think it is a problem.
Hey, Icicles, if you're having a problem with gravity.
You should have thought about that
Before you decided to live out on a limb.
Listen, even before I arrived,
You had to know everything is in flux,
Subject to change.
Change is the only thing that is constant.
Now you are worried that how it once was
Will not be the same forever and ever,
Calling it vulgar what is being done to this earth.

Icicles, you need to lighten up some.
Progress often looks vulgar / so unaccustomed we are
To real change, this change
That sometimes overcomes me, for I,
More than most, see everything from Icicles' point of view,
See man as short-sighted, often mean-spirited and greedy,
But I also see the goal of man as something good,
A paradise all can enjoy / and it is here

That Icicles usually stop me, saying it is me
Who has now climbed out on a limb.
They say my ideas about paradise are a bad joke,
That it was all a paradise before man arrived
And these ill-informed merry pranksters
Were only too happy to see it change.

62

Icicles do not fear being unpopular
And often are very objective about it,
Saying they were sure it was bound to happen
In a world that denies any absolute moral standard,
In a world that questions the desirability of the rule of law
Or any law which restricts man from obtaining
All that he thinks is rightfully his.
In fact, Icicles will tell you / hat being unpopular
Has had the opposite effect / It has made them stronger /
More determined to exist not on man's terms
But on the terms that nature has granted to them.
How classic,
Those with the least influence
The first to question the ultimate fulfillment
Of a civilized society / calling it barbaric,
Calling for a return to normalcy / for boundaries,
For permission to enter or change.
Icicles, who do they think they are,
God's favorite?

63

Icicles do not like to play the penitent,
Nor is it to their advantage to do so.
They are devotees of Artaud
And bristle at any suggestion
That they might have done something wrong.
Consider this an aid to their situation,
A paradigm of sorts / A van pulls up /
Of no particular age / and no identifiable features,
Yet immediately it is dissed.
To add to this dilemma, rocks are thrown at it.
Now you are the owner of the van
But not the driver / What are you to do?
Hope the driver returns? / Slim chance of that,
Not in this heat wave / Hope a paperhanger arrives
And covers the van with yesterday's newspaper?
Yeah, like that is really going to happen / How about
Telling the folks outside you are a song and dance man
And unless this barrage of rocks and abuse stops /
You will be forced from your van to do your act /
The always popular off-key rendition of / "When They Do
The Rumba, Down in Cuba on the Tuba" while at the same
Time performing a series of lackadaisical pirouettes / A real
Crowd pleaser, that one /

Folks, therein lie the difficulties
In being an Icicle / Prepare to be ruffled / because ruffled
You will be / There is no escaping it / You cannot bend
over,
Scrape the mud off your shoes / and pretend nothing happened /
It did / And don't suggest turning the other cheek / You will
Just get pounded on the other cheek / This stuff happens /
Icicles know it, and they know not to act the penitent,

To think somehow this is their fault / when it is not.
This why they like Artaud and the Theater of the Absurd.
For Icicles, life is absurd / cruel and not very cool,
So they learn to be stoics / watch from their perch
The theater of life / and secretly practice their
Pirouettes: step, lift, spin, spin.

64

Icicles have a rather bad habit
Of expecting a respectful burst of recognition
From those men or beasts
Who stumble out into the cold morning air
Either to fetch a nut or warm a car engine.
Icicles would like to see
A glow, a nod, a smile,
As if by magic, Spring had arrived
And Icicles were like flowers in first glorious bloom.
As Icicles contend, they contain the same amount of joy.
In a world full of vices this is such a minor one.
Icicles would do well to forgive and forget,
And they probably would
Except there are complications involved.

Icicles feel excluded, not worthy enough.
Then comes the resentment,
Then the "Why should we care?
You go about your business, we will go about ours."
And the world that cold winter's morn
Becomes that much colder and harder.

65

Icicles in galoshes,
Folks, I am telling you right now,
It just ain't right.
We should be ashamed of ourselves
For letting it happen.
Whether it is because of the dismay they feel
At reaching a certain age
Or the agitation caused
By knowing that no one really cares,
Seeing Icicles in galoshes,
Folks, something has got to be done.
And fast, cause I am seeing more and more each day.
At first, I'll admit I was rather taken in,
Thought it rather beguiling.
Later I thought it was some type of shtick,
A lot of sheen, followed up by some ahh shucks.

Now we know Icicles and Adorno
Have been spotted shambling around,
Each with a racing form in hand,
Saying the favorite never even showed up at the gate,
Mumbling that show business is over.
The man responsible for shoveling the shit has quit,
Saying today it is up to their knees
And by tomorrow it will only be worse,
And yes, this is the same Adorno
Who said, "Anyone who writes poetry after Auschwitz is
Barbaric." Now they are saying, "The barbarians are
Already here, now it is only a matter of who will win."

66

Icicles must quickly defamiliarize themselves
From the world about them.
This is done for protection / This is done by Dyne.
Dyne is a spiritual force necessary
To ward off the material world
In order to allow Icicles the strength and time
To create a whole in which they are the center.
This in turn allows them to become
An important part of the natural world.
Complicated, I know,
But to make matters worse,
Dyne is also a physical force.
It is the energy that gives Icicles an upward pull
And allows them to remain steady.
For Icicles, it is all about Dyne.

One should never underestimate the disparity
Between Icicles and the world at large.
It is the same disparity that drives man
To customize the world to suit his needs.
The psychological effect of wondering, "maybe
We do not belong here"
Is no different for Icicles than it is for man,
Except man has the ability to move from place to place,
To begin the challenge anew with experience gained
From previous attempts / to believe
That this time things will be better.
Icicles have no such choice.
The world which is new to them must immediately
Be put into a perspective that is clearly understandable.
If not / no Icicles / no need for Dyne.

67

In his writing, Kierkegaard suggested
That Icicles were the first and only true form
Of disintegration / cathartic in the realization
That change is not only a destructive principle
But a building force / In Icicles
Lay the groundwork of dreams dissolving energy,
Preparing the soil below for what is to come.
In Icicles is the faith necessary
To leave behind all we have first created,
Knowing what will come after comes from love.

In the past, I may have given Icicles advice
Which now I am not so proud of,
Advice with allegorical implications,
Advice about nocturnal collapse,
Advice concerning an improvised, warmer alter ego,
Advice which underlined the obvious:
That Icicles are a commodity not really in demand,
That Icicles needed to drop that earnest look
And go for a more down to earth, seedy, sensuous
Women-of-world look with a mysterious twist,
That Icicles need to abandon the pedantic
Screeching of fingernails across the blackboard
About this supposed hermetic relationship
Between men and Icicles / That what happens to one
Must happen to the other / Most men cannot make
Heads or tails of it / I thought I told them all this in a
Nice, polite way / but after I told them, they called me
An earthworm from Herzegovina / I said that was
Impossible because I had never been to Herzegovina,
But the Icicles just looked down on me with that
Cold, icy stare, impervious to all I had said / For what it is
Worth, I still think they are going about this all wrong /
And I believe I am correct in saying that I was the first
To suggest they use the heroic heretic approach.
Icicles, what else can I say / They make it so hard
To like them / Just like the rest of nature /
Stubborn to a fault / Unable or unwilling
To change in their ways.

69

It is oddly dignified and fairly evident
That Icicles have a firm constitution.
I believe this is due to their intricacy,
Their highly organized framework.
I am sure
Their caution and their excessive care
Are due to their acute awareness
Of their surrounding circumstances.
This being said,
You would think that Icicles would be boring.
Why the interest?
Daresay could it be
Because they are superior.

70

Often,
More often than one would suspect,
Icicles prefer old dilapidated farmhouses
To the more modern city ranch houses or bungalows.
I believe this is due to a subconscious disconnect
That Icicles have with the modern world.
Old farm houses that are in shambles,
Tenement houses on land gone to seed,
There Icicles have faith in their own industry,
That what they have created will not pass unnoticed,
That what is old was at one time new.
Icicles have small faith in the modern world,
A world that prides itself on how well
Everything and everyone is connected.
To Icicles, this world has lost its touch,
The touch of a human hand upon a face,
Or an Icicle pressed against a cheek.
Ordinarily, it may not seem like much.
Ordinarily, it should feel like a lot.

"Only a miracle can turn you right-side up"
Is a taunt / is one Icicle taunting another Icicle
Who seems squeamish about hanging upside-down.
Such taunts are uttered all the time
By Icicles / for whom time seems heavy
And hope that a little humor might lighten the load.
Maliciously, certainly, but I should add
That their favorite targets are humans.
"Why not stay awhile, enjoy the fine weather?"
A jeer like that will send a row of Icicles into hysterics,
Then the barbs come fast and furious.
"No need to run, we are not going to chase you."
"Yeah, you are our kind, you are too ugly."
From there, the humor degrades into personal attacks.
"Yeah, two-legged ugly / Yeah, but butt ugly."
Then the final crowning glory: "You call that a head
On your shoulders, I don't see any point!"
Childish, juvenile humor, but Icicles revel in it.
It is Icicles enjoying being Icicles / though I know
Any respect you had for Icicles is now gone.
So be it. It is only natural that Icicles are not sensitive.
It is a hostile world they live in / under the afternoon sun,
When every drop hurts / Icicles will look at one another
And say, "You don't look so hot."
"Well, I feel like I am burning up.
I feel like I need to rest in the shade below."
"Bad idea, always a bad idea to drop everything.
Stay with me for a while, I think I see more humans."
For Icicles, that act is in the acting
And as any good actor knows, you have to practice.

Sadly, Icicles correspond not so much with life's amenities,
Though they are certainly one of life's more pleasant
Features, but more and more Icicles find themselves
Associated with what we see as illicit and elusive,
Objects that are forfeited or in need of an imprimatur.
Certainly, it cannot be argued that Icicles are found
Only in the Winter, but is this because of some sort of
Sanction that Icicles have agreed to, and by agreeing
To this sanction did they also forfeit any hope
For universal love and admiration? This feature alone
Makes Icicles seem elusive, mysterious,
Hard to understand. Why would they ever agree
To pay such a heavy price for so little of an advantage?
Is it because Icicles have done something illicit, wrong,
An evil so bad that they were banished to the darkest
Season? None of this would be of any importance
If Icicles did not look so pure and innocent,
Not that I or any human would want to imply
That such an evil did occur. Yet it does seem suspicious.
Are Icicles the work of the devil, and if so, is man
Correct in his war, a holy war, to cast out evil?
Ah, the mind of men.
Icicles never cease to wonder at it.
Always some conspiracy,
Always their rights are threatened.
True, it is bad for Icicles, but even worse for men.

73

At this point, you're thinking
Icicles are narcoleptic and narcissistic,
A little bit too dopey
To be the real hero in this narrative.
What this story needs is some undercover narcs,
Drug cartels run by evil foreigners,
Or better yet, a spy murder mystery.
Our agent will be a leggy, slinky blonde.
The bad guys can resemble Boris and Natasha,
But be careful here, Russia is about to be our new ally.
Let's have a few explosions and one wild car chase scene.
Nevertheless,
There is a real emergency happening right now
And the call to 911 keeps going unanswered.
Ultimately, something is going to have to be done,
But for now, as for the narcolepsy,
It is not the Icicles who have it.

74

The only things Icicles are victims of
Is preemptive paranoia.
All of this is overheated exaggeration.
I, too, might sound creepy
If I had been squeezed, then frozen.
The result is all gloom and doom.
Behind all this hype,
What Icicles really want
Is to be today's Pop-tastic.

Okay, so you are afraid,
Afraid this might be the end of homo-superior.
Hey, all good things must end,
But to postpone it a bit,
You might want to consider Pascal's wager.
Simple enough: clean up the environment.
What do you have to lose?
If global warming is a hoax,
Then you have a clean environment,
Not a bad thing.
But if it is not a hoax
And mother earth is really warming, dangerously so,
You are at least working to fix the mess.
Oh, this wager will cost a lot of money,
That's the real problem, isn't it.
Well, the answer to that is also simple:
End the arms race, stop all military spending.
Call it individual interest in the common good
Over nationalistic interest in total annihilation.
And the good thing is, as soon as this crisis is over,
You can go right back to where you left off.

Notes

Notes

Notes

Notes

Notes

Notes

Notes

About the Author

P. W. Lea is a native of Nashville, Tennessee.
Is a graduate of the University of Tennessee, Knoxville.
Moved to Berkeley, California, where he was a member of
The Berkeley Poet's Cooperative. He writes and lives in
Nashville, Tennessee, and is the author of several plays,
stories and poems.

Icicles on Christine's Front Porch

ISBN: 978-0-578-40821-7

www.ingramcontent.com/pod-product-compliance
Lightning Source LLC
Chambersburg PA
CBHW060952040426
42445CB00011B/1123